WE KNOW THE
ABCs
OF BLACK HISTORY...DO YOU?
Volume 1

"WE KNOW THE ABCs OF BLACK HISTORY...DO YOU?" was created to change the false narrative taught in schools for generations...and that is that the Black American story is just one of oppression. Nothing could be further from the truth.

So much of Black history has been hidden, omitted or whitewashed to the point where most Americans, as well as people around the world, are completely unaware of the many inventions, innovations, contributions and heroics of Black Americans throughout American history.

This book can be read to children as young as 2, and as they grow and learn to read, it can be a continued source of learning. Knowledge is POWER!

It was important that the information in this book was simplified for easy comprehension without talking down or brushing over importantly needed facts.

Published By MSW Books
Knowledge Is Power

WE KNOW THE
ABCs
OF BLACK HISTORY...DO YOU?
Volume 1

Published By MSW Books
Knowledge Is Power

copyright 2024

First Edition

Written and Designed by Maurice Woodson

One must know where they come from in order to know where they are going.

We are inventors, innovators, explorers, heroes, educators, scientists, leaders and so much more.

knowledge is power!

WE KNOW THE ABCs OF BLACK HISTORY... DO YOU?

Volume 1

A

WE KNOW THE ABCs OF BLACK HISTORY AND WE ARE GOING TO SHARE WHAT WE KNOW WITH YOU. I'M GOING TO START WITH THE LETTER "A".

ALFRED L. CRALLE

HE INVENTED AND PATENTED THE ICE CREAM SCOOP ON FEBRUARY 2, 1897. EVERY TIME YOU WATCH SOMEONE SCOOP ICE CREAM INTO A BOWL OR CONE, YOU CAN THANK MR. CRALLE.

ALICE PARKER

SHE, IN 1918, CREATED AND PATENTED AN INDOOR HEATING FURNACE THAT COULD BE USED TO HEAT AN ENTIRE HOME.

THE WORD "PATENT" IS USED OFTEN HERE, SO I WANTED TO TAKE A MOMENT TO EXPLAIN WHAT IT IS. A PATENT IS A RIGHT GRANTED TO AN INVENTOR BY THE FEDERAL GOVERNMENT THAT PERMITS THE INVENTOR EXCLUSIVE RIGHTS. THESE RIGHTS EXCLUDE OTHERS FROM MAKING, SELLING, OR USING THE INVENTION WITHOUT PERMISSION.
OKAY, NOW FOR MORE ABCs OF BLACK HISTORY.

ALEXANDRIA LIBRARY SIT-IN

THE ALEXANDRIA LIBRARY SIT-IN WAS ONE OF THE FIRST PEACEFUL PROTEST OF ITS TYPE IN THE AMERICA. IT WAS USED TO FIGHT AGAINST DISCRIMINATION AND HATE.

IT TOOK PLACE ON AUGUST 21,1939

ALLEN ALLENSWORTH,

ALLEN ALLENSWORTH WAS A MILITARY CLERGYMAN COLONEL, WHO FOUNDED A BLACK TOWN IN CALIFORNIA IN 1908. IN THIS TOWN, BLACK AMERICANS WERE ABLE TO RUN THEIR OWN BUSINESSES, SCHOOLS AND GOVERNMENT. THE TOWN THRIVED UNTIL THE STATE, HOPING TO FORCE PEOPLE OUT, DIVERTED WATER FROM IT, CAUSING DROUGHTS. THE STATE THEN REMOVED THE TRAIN STATION, MAKING IT NEARLY IMPOSSIBLE TO TRAVEL AS NEEDED OR FOR OTHERS TO REACH THEM.

B

BENJAMIN BRADLEY

HE DEVELOPED A STEAM ENGINE FOR WAR SHIPS. HE UNFAIRLY WAS NOT ALLOWED TO PATENT HIS CREATION, SO HE WAS FORCED TO SELL WHAT HE CREATED FOR LESS THAN IT WAS WORTH.

BENJAMIN BANNEKER

HE TAUGHT HIMSELF MATHEMATICS AND ASTRONOMY. HE CREATED AN ALMANAC BASED ON HIS ASTRONOMICAL CALCULATIONS AND FORECAST HIS FIRST LUNAR ECLIPSE IN 1789. MR. BANNEKER WAS ALSO AN ARCHITECT WHO, IN 1779, HELPED, MAP, SURVEY AND DESIGN WASHINGTON D.C., HOME OF THE WHITE HOUSE AND FEDERAL GOVERNMENT.

BLACK PANTHER PARTY

THE BLACK PANTHER PARTY, NOT TO BE MISTAKEN FOR THE SUPERHERO, WAS AN ORGANIZATION THAT DID MANY GOOD AND HEROIC THINGS INCLUDING PROTECTING THOSE IN NEED, CREATING FREE SCHOOL BREAKFAST PROGRAMS FOR 20,000 CHILDREN, AND THEY ALSO PROVIDED FREE MEDICAL CLINICS AND AMBULANCE SERVICES.

BLANCHE KELSO BRUCE

HE WAS THIRD TO WIN A CONGRESSIONAL SEAT, BUT FIRST TO SERVE A FULL TERM IN THE SENATE. HE SERVED FROM 1875 TO 1881. IN 1880 HE WAS THE FIRST TO BE NOMINATED AS VICE PRESIDENT.

BENJAMIN O. DAVIS JR.

HE BECAME THE FIRST BLACK AMERICAN GENERAL IN THE U.S. AIR FORCE IN 1954.

C

CHARLES HENRY TURNER
CHARLES HENRY TURNER RECEIVED SEVERAL COLLEGE DEGREES BETWEEN 1891 AND 1907. BECAUSE OF HIS STUDIES, HE KNEW MORE ABOUT THE BEHAVIOR OF INSECTS THAN ANYONE. MR. TURNER WAS THE FIRST RESEARCHER TO PROVE THAT INSECTS CAN HEAR.
CRISPUS ATTUCKS
CRISPUS ATTUCKS, WHO WAS OF AFRICAN AND INDIGENOUS NATIVE INDIAN DESCENT, WAS A HERO. AS THE AMERICAN REVOLUTION BEGAN IN BOSTON, MR. ATTUCKS HEROICALLY WAS THE FIRST PERSON TO STAND UP AND FIGHT. OTHERS THEN FOLLOWED HIS LEAD.
CARTER G. WOODSON
FRUSTRATED THAT BLACK HISTORY WASN'T BEING TAUGHT, CARTER G. WOODSON CREATED WHAT WAS THEN CALLED BLACK HISTORY WEEK, WHICH LATER BECAME KNOWN AS BLACK HISTORY MONTH.

CHARLES DREW

DR. CHARLES DREW WAS A LEADING RESEARCHER IN THE FIELD OF BLOOD STORAGE AND PRESERVATION. HE PIONEERED THE BLOOD TRANSFUSION AND LED A MASSIVE BLOOD DONATION DRIVE TO PROVIDE MUCH-NEEDED BLOOD SUPPLIES DURING WORLD WAR II. KNOWN AS THE "FATHER OF BLOOD BANKING," MR. DREW'S LEGACY IS STILL FELT TODAY WHENEVER THE RED CROSS SAVES LIVES, BECAUSE HE LAID THE GROUNDWORK.

CIVIL RIGHTS ACT OF 1866

THE VOTING RIGHTS ACT OF 1866 WAS THE FIRST FEDERAL LAW TO DEFINE CITIZENSHIP AND AFFIRM THAT ALL CITIZENS ARE EQUAL AND PROTECTED BY THE LAW, HOWEVER, IT ALSO BLOCKED BLACK AMERICANS FROM VOTING. MY MOTHER WOULD CALL THAT A CONTRADICTION. HOW CAN YOU BE AN EQUAL CITIZEN, BUT NOT BE ALLOWED TO VOTE?

I HAVE ONE MORE.
CHARLES JACKSON FRENCH
ON SEPTEMBER 5, 1942, HE SWAM THROUGH SHARK INFESTED WATERS FOR 6 TO 8 HOURS, PULLING A RAFT OF 15 WOUNDED NAVY SOLDIERS, SAVING THEM FROM A SINKING SHIP DURING WW2. CHARLES JACKSON FRENCH WAS NOT ONLY A HERO, HE WAS A GREAT SWIMMER. HE RECEIVED A MEDAL FOR HIS HEROISM IN 1943.

D

DANIEL HALE WILLIAMS

DR. DANIEL HALE WILLIAMS WAS BORN IN PENNSYLVANIA AND ATTENDED MEDICAL SCHOOL IN CHICAGO, WHERE HE RECEIVED HIS M.D. IN 1883. HE FOUNDED THE PROVIDENT HOSPITAL IN CHICAGO IN 1891, THE OLDEST FREE-STANDING BLACK-OWNED HOSPITAL IN THE UNITED STATES. DR. WILLIAMS WAS ALSO THE FIRST DOCTOR OF ANY RACE TO SUCCESSFULLY PERFORM OPEN HEART SURGERY. HIS TECHNIQUES ARE STILL STUDIED TODAY.

IN 1968, DIAHANN CARROLL BECAME THE FIRST AFRICAN AMERICAN WOMAN TO HAVE HER OWN WEEKLY TELEVISION SERIES, "JULIA." MY GRANDMOTHER LOVED AND CONTINUOUSLY TALKED ABOUT THAT SHOW.

DAVID CROSTHWAIT

DAVID CROSTHWAIT, JR. WAS AN EXPERT IN HEATING, VENTILATION, AND AIR CONDITIONING. HE DESIGNED THE HEATING SYSTEM FOR RADIO CITY MUSIC HALL IN NEW YORK. DURING HIS LIFETIME HE RECEIVED MORE THAN 40 U.S. PATENTS RELATING TO HEATING, VENTILATION AND AIR CONDITIONING SYSTEMS.

E

ESTEVANICO DE DORANTES PARTICIPATED IN AN EXPLORATION FROM MEXICO INTO NORTH AMERICA IN 1540. DURING HIS EXPLORATIONS HE DISCOVERED THE TERRITORY THAT WOULD BECOME ARIZONA AND NEW MEXICO.

EMITT MCHENRY.

MR. MCHENRY CREATED A COMPLEX CODE WHICH ALLOWS ANY PERSON THE ABILITY TO SEARCH THE INTERNET AND USE EMAIL. WHAT HE CREATED IS WHAT WE NOW KNOW AS .COM AND .NET

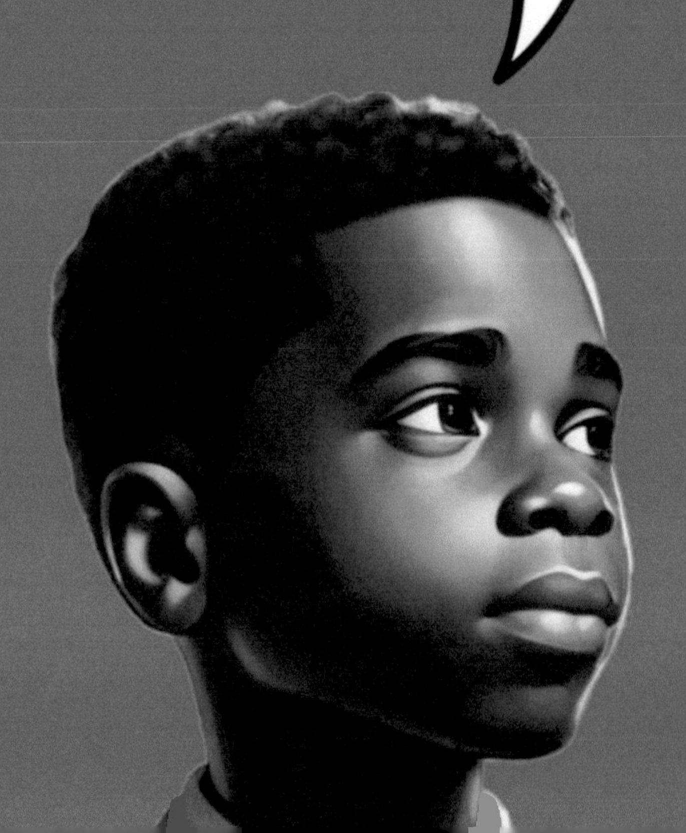

EATONVILLE

EATONVILLE IS THE OLDEST TOWN IN THE UNITED STATES TO BE FOUNDED AND INCORPORATED BY AN AFRICAN AMERICAN. IT WAS FOUNDED ON AUGUST 5, 1887 IN FLORIDA.

EDWARD ALEXANDER BOUCHET

MR. BOUCHET WAS THE FIRST BLACK AMERICAN OR AS I PREFER TO SAY, AFRICAN AMERICAN TO GRADUATE FROM YALE COLLEGE. HE GRADUATED IN 1874. IN 1876, HE RECEIVED HIS PH.D. , BECOMING THE FIRST AFRICAN AMERICAN TO EARN A DOCTORATE. BOUCHET SPENT HIS CAREER TEACHING COLLEGE CHEMISTRY AND PHYSICS.

FRANK WILLIS

FRANK WILLIS, A BLACK AMERICAN SECURITY GUARD, WAS THE PERSON WHO DISCOVERED PRESIDENT NIXON'S COVER-UP WHICH LATER CAUSED HIS RESIGNATION AS PRESIDENT OF THE UNITED STATES.

FREDRICK DOUGLASS

THERE IS A LOT TO SAY ABOUT FREDRICK DOUGLASS, BUT ONE RARELY MENTIONED FACT IS THAT HE WAS THE FIRST BLACK AMERICAN TO RUN FOR PRESIDENT OF THE UNITED STATES IN 1888. HE WAS ALSO THE FIRST TO BE PUT ON THE TICKET AS VICE-PRESIDENT IN 1872 BY VICTORIA WOODHULL, THE FIRST WOMAN TO RUN FOR PRESIDENT.

FREDERICK MCKINLEY JONES

THE REASON WHY FRESH FOOD CAN BE TRUCKED AND SHIPPED FROM ACROSS THE COUNTRY TO YOUR LOCAL SUPERMARKET, IS BECAUSE OF AN AFRICAN AMERICAN INVENTOR NAMED FREDERICK MCKINLEY JONES. YOU CAN THANK HIM. HE INVENTED THE AIR-COOLING UNITS USED IN FOOD TRANSPORTING TRUCKS IN THE 1930s, AND WAS AWARDED MORE THAN 60 PATENTS OVER THE COURSE OF HIS LIFE, 40 OF WHICH INVOLVED REFRIGERATION EQUIPMENT.

GRANVILLE T. WOODS

GRANVILLE TAILER WOODS WAS A BLACK AMERICAN INVENTOR WHO MADE SIGNIFICANT CONTRIBUTIONS TO THE TELEPHONE, TELEGRAPH, TRANSPORTATION SAFETY AND AUTOMOTIVE TECHNOLOGY, AND WHOSE GENIUS STILL AFFECTS DEVICES WE USE TODAY.

GEORGE EDWIN TAYLOR

IN 1904, HE BECAME THE SECOND BLACK AMERICAN TO RUN FOR PRESIDENT.

COL. GUION S. BLUFORD, JR.

HE WAS AN ASTRONAUT. HE WAS THE FIRST BLACK AMERICAN IN SPACE. HE HAS GONE INTO SPACE 4 TIMES.

GARRETT AUGUSTUS MORGAN

GARRETT AUGUSTUS MORGAN INVENTED A SMOKE HOOD IN 1916 THAT HE USED TO RESCUE SEVERAL MEN TRAPPED BY AN EXPLOSION IN TUNNELS UNDER LAKE ERIE. THIS INVENTION WAS LATER REFINED BY THE U.S. ARMY INTO THE GAS MASK, WHICH WAS USED TO PROTECT SOLDIERS FROM CHLORINE FUMES DURING WORLD WAR I. HE ALSO INVENTED AN EARLY VERSION OF A TRAFFIC SIGNAL THAT FEATURED AUTOMATED STOP AND GO SIGNS.

GEORGE WASHINGTON CARVER

GEORGE WASHINGTON CARVER WAS A SCIENTIST, A TEACHER, AND INVENTOR. HE HELPED FORD MOTOR COMPANY CREATE A RUBBER SUBSTITUTE WHICH WAS USED ON CARS AND HE ALSO CREATED OVER 300 PRODUCTS USING PEANUTS, 118 PRODUCTS FROM SWEET POTATOES AND 75 FROM PECANS. THE ONE THING HE DIDN'T CREATE WAS PEANUT BUTTER, EVEN THOUGH SCHOOLS AROUND THE COUNTRY TEACH THAT HE DID. HE DID HOWEVER, CREATE SO MANY OTHER AMAZING THINGS. WE SHOULD ALL LEARN ABOUT ALL OF THE AMAZING THINGS THAT HE CREATED. SOME WILL SURPRISE YOU. THEY INCLUDE: FOODS, MEDICINES, BEVERAGES, PAINTS, SOAP & CLEANSERS, PAPER, INK, RUBBER, GASOLINE, INSECTICIDE, GLUE AND MORE.

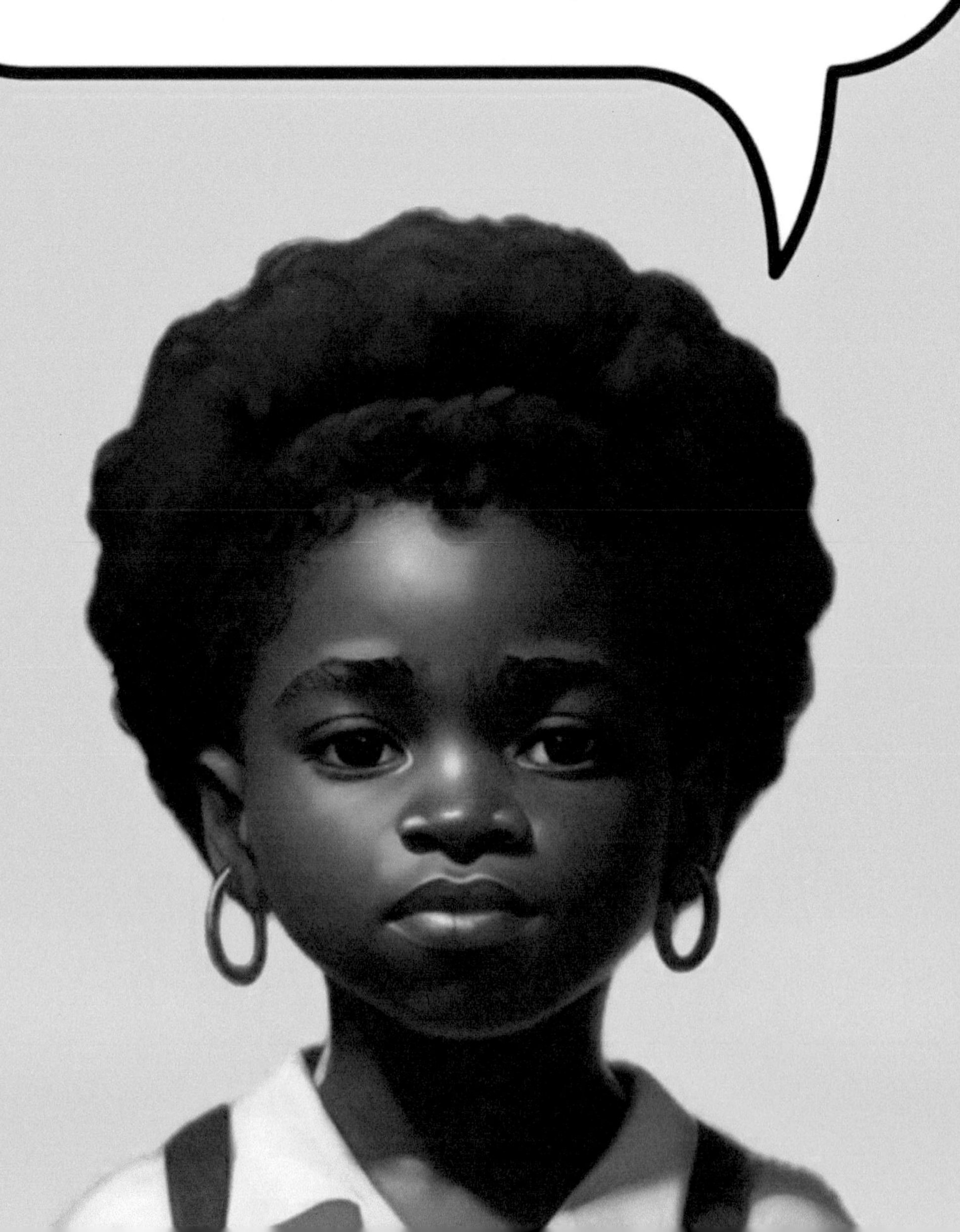

GEORGE (CRUM) SPECK

GEORGE (CRUM) SPECK, A CHEF, INVENTED THE POTATO CHIP WHEN HE ACCIDENTALLY DROPPED A THIN CUT POTATO INTO OIL. AFTER REMOVING IT, SEASONING IT, AND TASTING IT, HE DECIDED THAT IT WAS SO GOOD THAT HE WAS GOING TO SERVE IT TO CUSTOMERS AS A SPECIAL TREAT. IT BECAME SO POPULAR THAT PEOPLE BEGAN SHOWING UP AT THE RESTAURANT JUST TO BUY THE POTATO CHIPS.

I THINK I'M HUNGRY NOW.

HENRY T SAMPSON
MR. SAMPSON WAS AN INVENTOR AND TECHNOLOGY PIONEER. HE HOLDS MANY PATENTS USED IN THE CREATION OF THE ORIGINAL CELL PHONE AND IS ALSO AN ACTUAL EXPERT IN ROCKET SCIENCE. HIS INVENTIONS AND PATENTS POWERED ROCKETS AND SPACE SATELLITES.

HENRY A. JACKSON

ALTHOUGH THE INVENTION OF WHAT COULD BE CALLED A TABLE GOES BACK FAR IN HISTORY, THE MODERN DAY HOME KITCHEN TABLE WAS INVENTED AND PATENTED BY BLACK AMERICA INVENTOR HENRY A. JACKSON. HIS INVENTION WAS NOT JUST FOR EATING ON, IT ALSO HAD STORAGE SPACE FOR POTS AND KITCHEN UTENSILS. TODAY THE KITCHEN ISLAND AND KITCHEN DINING TABLE ARE BOTH DERIVED FROM HIS CREATION.

HENRIETTA LACKS

HER CELLS TISSUE WAS REMOVED WITHOUT HER KNOWLEDGE AND RESEARCHED AFTER IT WAS DISCOVERED TO BE EXTRAORDINARY. AS A RESULT HER CELLS WERE THE BASIS TO CREATE DISEASE CURES AND MANY VACCINES, SUCH AS THE VACCINE FOR POLIO AND COVID-19.

INDEPENDENCE HEIGHTS

BLACK FAMILIES STARTED TO MIGRATE TO AN AREA IN NORTHERN HOUSTON KNOWN AS THE INDEPENDENCE HEIGHTS AROUND 1908. THE AREA WAS DEVELOPED AND CONSISTED OF SMALL WOOD-FRAME HOUSES. MANY OF THE HOUSES WERE BUILT BY BLACK BUILDING CONTRACTORS WHO LIVED IN THE AREA.

ON JANUARY 25, 1915, INDEPENDENCE HEIGHTS, WITH A POPULATION OF NEARLY 600 WAS INCORPORATED, BECOMING THE FIRST BLACK AMERICAN TOWN IN TEXAS.

IDA B. WELLS-BARNETT.

IDA B. WELLS-BARNETT, A PERSONAL HERO OF MINE, WAS A PROMINENT JOURNALIST, ACTIVIST, AND RESEARCHER, IN THE LATE 19TH AND EARLY 20TH CENTURIES. AS A SKILLED WRITER, MRS. WELLS-BARNETT ALSO USED HER TALENT AS A JOURNALIST TO SHED LIGHT ON THE CONDITIONS OF AFRICAN AMERICANS THROUGHOUT THE SOUTH. IN HER LIFETIME, SHE BATTLED SEXISM, RACISM, AND VIOLENCE. UNFORTUNATELY THINGS THAT STILL EXISTS TODAY.

J

JEFFERSON FRANKLIN LONG WAS THE FIRST BLACK PERSON TO SPEAK IN THE HOUSE OF REPRESENTATIVES AS A CONGRESSMAN IN 1871.

JEAN BAPTISTE POINT DU SABLE,

HE WAS A BLACK AMERICAN FROM SAINTE-DOMINGUE HAITI. HE BUILT THE FIRST PERMANENT SETTLEMENT IN WHAT WOULD BECOME CHICAGO IN 1779.

JOHN LEE LOVE

JOHN LEE LOVE INVENTED THE HAND CRANKED PENCIL SHARPENER. MY SCHOOL STILL HAS THOSE IN MOST CLASSES.

JOHN STANDARD

MR. STANDARD INVENTED THE SPACE SAVING OIL BURNING STOVE, WHICH INSPIRED THE MODERN STOVE. HE ALSO PERFECTED THE ICE BOX, MAKING A MUCH IMPROVED REFRIGERATOR FROM THE CRUDE VERSION THAT CAME BEFORE. HE IS CALLED THE FATHER OF THE MODERN DAY REFRIGERATOR.

JESSE OWENS

JESSE OWENS BROKE 4 WORLD RECORDS IN ONE AFTERNOON AT THE BIG TEN CHAMPIONSHIPS ON MAY 25, 1935 A YEAR LATER, HE UPSTAGED ADOLF HITLER BY WINNING 4 GOLD MEDALS (100 METER, 200 METER, 4 TIMES 100 METER RELAY AND LONG JUMP) AT THE 1936 OLYMPICS IN BERLIN.

JACK JOHNSON

JACK JOHNSON WAS THE FIRST BLACK AMERICAN HEAVYWEIGHT BOXING CHAMPION IN 1907. DUE TO HIS LOVE OF CARPENTRY, HE ALSO PATENTED AN IMPROVEMENT ON THE WRENCH

ON APRIL 18, 1928.

JERRY LAWSON.

JERRY LAWSON, IN 1970, CREATED THE FIRST VIDEO-GAME TO USE CARTRIDGES. HIS WORK BECAME THE FOUNDATION FOR COMPANIES LIKE; ATARI, NINTENDO AND XBOX.

I GUESS YOU CAN SAY HE CHANGED THE GAME.

THAT WAS MY DAD'S JOKE. WE PLAY A LOT OF VIDEO GAMES TOGETHER.

JESSE RUSSELL

IN 1988, JESSE RUSSELL LED THE FIRST TEAM TO INTRODUCE DIGITAL CELLULAR TECHNOLOGY. HE HAS CREATED AND PATENTED DOZENS OF INNOVATIONS IN WIRELESS TECHNOLOGY, INCLUDING BASE STATION TECHNOLOGY, WHICH TRANSMITS RADIO WAVE SIGNALS TO AND FROM MOBILE DEVICES. HIS OTHER PATENTS INCLUDE: "BASE STATION FOR MOBILE RADIO TELECOMMUNICATIONS SYSTEMS", THE "MOBILE DATA TELEPHONE", AND THE "WIRELESS COMMUNICATION BASE".

WITHOUT JESSE RUSSELL WE WOULD NOT HAVE THESE SMART PHONES WE USE EVERYDAY TO PLAY GAMES, WATCH MOVIES AND SKITS, VIDEO CHAT OR TO SO MANY OTHER THINGS. I LEARN MORE AND MORE THAT THERE ARE SO MANY THINGS THAT IMPACT OUR LIVES THAT COME FROM BLACK INGENUITY. WHY DON'T THEY TEACH ANY OF THIS IN SCHOOL? I GUESS THAT'S A QUESTION FOR ANOTHER TIME.

KAMALA HARRIS.
KAMALA HARRIS, WHO I ADMIRE SO MUCH, IS A POLITICIAN AND ATTORNEY.
SHE IS THE 49TH VICE PRESIDENT OF THE UNITED STATES. IT MAKES HER, NOT ONLY THE FIRST BLACK AMERICAN WOMAN AND WOMAN OF COLOR TO BECOME VICE PRESIDENT, SHE IS ALSO THE FIRST WOMAN IN HISTORY TO HOLD THAT POSITION.

KENNY STANLEY WASHINGTON

KENNY STANLEY WASHINGTON ALSO KNOWN BY HIS NICKNAME "KINGFISH" WAS THE FIRST BLACK AMERICAN TO SIGN A CONTRACT TO PLAY FOR THE NFL.

BEFORE THE NFL, HE PLAYED COLLEGE FOOTBALL FOR THE UCLA BRUINS IN LOS ANGELES, CALIFORNIA. HE ALSO PLAYED BASEBALL FOR UCLA ALONGSIDE JACKIE ROBINSON.

L

LOUIS LATIMER

LOUIS LATIMER WAS THE ONLY AFRICAN AMERICAN ENGINEER AND SCIENTIST TO BE PART OF THE ELITE EDISON PIONEERS RESEARCH AND DEVELOPMENT ORGANIZATION. BEFORE LATIMER'S INTERVENTION AND INVOLVEMENT, EDISON'S LIGHT BULBS WAS A FAILURE AND WOULD BURN ONLY FOR A FEW MINUTES. MR. LATIMER'S INGENUITY LED TO THE CREATION OF THE CARBON FILAMENT WHICH ALLOWED LIGHT BULBS TO BURN FOR HOURS. IT IS WHY WE HAVE LIGHTS IN OUR HOMES TODAY. HE ALSO CONTRIBUTED TO AND DRAFTED THE TELEPHONE FOR ALEXANDER GRAHAM BELL.

HIS OTHER INVENTIONS INCLUDE THE TOILET FOR TRAINS IN 1874 AND AN EARLY VERSION OF THE AIR CONDITIONER IN 1886.

LONNIE JOHNSON

LONNIE JOHNSON WAS EMPLOYED AS A NUCLEAR ENGINEER AND WAS AN AEROSPACE SCIENTIST. HE WORKED ON TECHNOLOGY AND JET PROPULSION FOR SPACE TRAVEL HE WAS PART OF THE TEAM THAT WORKED ON THE GALILEO MISSION TO JUPITER.

HE IS ALSO THE INVENTOR OF ONE OF MY FAVORITE THINGS...THE SUPER SOAKER WATER GUN, WHICH IS THE BEST SELLING TOY OF ALL TIME.

MATTHEW HENSON,

HE WAS A BLACK EXPLORER WHO ACCOMPANIED ADMIRAL ROBERT E. PEARY ON THE FIRST SUCCESSFUL EXPEDITION TO THE NORTH POLE IN 1909. MR. HENSON WAS ACTUALLY THE FIRST TO REACH THE NORTH POLES AND WAITED HOURS FOR PEARY TO CATCH UP AND JOIN HIM.

MARIE V. BRITTAN-BROWN

MARIE V. BRITTAN-BROWN WAS A FEMALE AFRICAN AMERICAN INVENTOR. SHE DESIGNED THE FIRST HOME SECURITY SYSTEM WHICH WAS PATENTED ON DECEMBER 2, 1969.

M.C. HARNEY

M.C. HARNEY WAS AN AFRICAN AMERICAN INVENTOR, WHO WHEN EVERYONE WAS USING CANDLES AT NIGHTS AS THE PRIMARY LIGHT SOURCE, USING HIS INGENUITY, HE INVENTED THE LANTERN LIGHT ON AUGUST 19, 1884.

MARK DEAN

COMPUTERS AS WE KNOW THEM WOULDN'T EXIST IF NOT FOR DR. MARK DEAN. ONE THIRD OF THE TECHNOLOGY USED ON THE ORIGINAL HOME COMPUTER WAS CREATED BY HIM.

N

NINA SIMONE

NINA SIMONE WAS A SINGER, SONGWRITER, PIANIST, AND MUSIC COMPOSER. SHE WAS GIFTED AND LEARNED TO PLAY THE PIANO AT 3 YEARS OLD. HER MUSIC CROSSED SEVERAL GENRES SUCH AS: JAZZ, BLUES, FOLK, GOSPEL, POP, SOUL, AND RHYTHM AND BLUES. SHE WAS ALSO A CIVIL RIGHTS ACTIVIST. HER ACTIVISM BEGAN WHEN SHE STARTED PROTESTING AT THE AGE OF 12. MUCH OF HER MUSIC ADDRESSED RACIAL AND SOCIAL INJUSTICE. ONE OF HER MOST FAMOUS ACTIVISM ANTHEMS WAS "TO BE YOUNG, GIFTED AND BLACK".

O

OTIS BOYKIN

OTIS BOYKIN'S MOST NOTEWORTHY INVENTION WAS AN ELECTRICAL MECHANISM, CREATED IN 1955, AS A REGULATING UNIT FOR THE HEART PACEMAKER. MY GRANDFATHER HAS A PACEMAKER SO THANK YOU MR. BOYKIN. MR. BOYKIN ALSO INVENTED A TYPE OF RESISTOR (AN ELECTRIC CIRCUIT ELEMENT) COMMONLY IN USE TODAY IN RADIOS, COMPUTERS, AND TELEVISION SETS.

OSCAR MICHEAUX

OSCAR MICHEAUX.WAS THE FIRST MAJOR MOVIE FILMMAKER. HIS WORK SHOWED A POSITIVE PORTRAYAL OF BLACK AMERICANS IN A TIME OF STEREOTYPE AND NEGATIVE CHARACTERS PORTRAYALS WERE THE NORM. HE DIRECTED AND PRODUCED 44 FILMS. MR. MICHEAUX WAS ONE OF THE MOST INFLUENTIAL FILMMAKERS OF HIS TIME.

PAUL ROBESON

PAUL ROBESON WAS A SINGER, ACTOR, PROFESSIONAL FOOTBALL STAR AND ACTIVIST. AS AN ACTOR HE FIRST STARRED IN SILENT FILMS, BUT REALLY MADE A NAME FOR HIMSELF WHEN SOUND ARRIVED. HE WAS INTENTIONAL ON STRIVING TO ALWAYS PROJECT POSITIVE IMAGES OF BLACK CHARACTERS.

PATRICIA BATH

DR. PATRICIA BATH INVENTED LASERPHACO, A NEW DEVICE AND TECHNIQUE THAT USES LASERS TO REMOVE CATARACTS. IT PERFORMED ALL STEPS OF CATARACT REMOVAL: MAKING THE INCISION, DESTROYING THE LENS AND VACUUMING OUT THE FRACTURED PIECES. BATH IS RECOGNIZED AS THE FIRST BLACK WOMAN PHYSICIAN TO RECEIVE A MEDICAL PATENT.

PHILIP. B DOWNING

DID YOU KNOW THAT WHEN YOU PUT MAIL INTO THE MAILBOX, YOU HAVE BLACK AMERICAN INVENTOR PHILIP DOWNING TO THANK FOR IT. IN 1891 HE CREATED AND PATENTED WHAT HE CALLED THE STREET LETTER BOX. TODAY WE SIMPLY CALL IT A MAILBOX. BEFORE HIS CREATION PEOPLE HAD TO TRAVEL TO THE POST OFFICE.

PHILIP EMEAGWALI

MR. EMEAGWALI IS KNOWN AS THE FATHER OF THE INTERNET BECAUSE HE USED WHAT HE KNEW OF HOW BEES CREATE HONEYCOMBS TO CREATE THE WORLDS FASTEST COMPUTER. BECAUSE HIS COMPUTERS COULD PERFORM 3.1 BILLION COMPUTATIONS PER SECOND, IT BECAME THE FOUNDATION OF WHICH THE INTERNET WAS BUILT. THERE WOULD BE NO SOCIAL MEDIA WITHOUT HIS CONTRIBUTION.

Q

QUINCY JONES

QUINCY JONES IS ONE OF THE MOST SUCCESSFUL MUSICIANS AND MUSIC PRODUCERS OF ALL TIME. HE HAS PRODUCED MUSIC FOR TOP ARTISTS FROM ALL GENRES INCLUDING: BLUES, JAZZ, RHYTHM AND BLUES, COUNTRY, POP, AND ROCK. HES ALSO PRODUCED AWARD WINNING FILMS, DOCUMENTARIES AND TELEVISION SHOWS.

QUINN BROWN

QUINN BROWN MADE A NAME FOR HERSELF DURING WOMEN'S SUFFRAGE IN THE EARLY 20TH CENTURY. MS. BROWN WAS ALSO A NOTABLE ORATOR AND AUTHOR, PUBLISHING A BOOK FOCUSING ON THE ACHIEVEMENTS OF BLACK WOMEN OF HER ERA. MS. BROWN DEVELOPED A REPUTATION AS A FORCEFUL SPEAKER, AND IN 1893 SHE USED HER GIFTS TO ORGANIZE THE COLORED WOMEN 'S LEAGUE OF WASHINGTON, D.C.

RECONSTRUCTION ERA

THE RECONSTRUCTION ERA LASTED FROM 1861 TO 1877. IT WAS CONSIDERED THE PERIOD OF LEGAL, POLITICAL AND SOCIAL RECREATION FOLLOWING THE CIVIL WAR. DURING THIS TIME SO MANY THINGS HAPPENED. THE CIVIL RIGHTS ACT OF 1866 WAS PASSED. IT WAS THE FIRST LAW TO DEFINE BLACK AMERICAN CITIZENSHIP AND AFFIRM THAT ALL WERE EQUAL UNDER THE LAW...AT LEAST THAT IS WHAT THE LAW SAID. UNFORTUNATELY, THE COUNTRY NEVER FULLY LIVED UP TO THAT. THE FIRST BLACK AMERICAN TO BE ELECTED AND SERVE IN CONGRESS HAPPENED DURING RECONSTRUCTION. HIS NAME WAS HIRAM RHODES. DID YOU KNOW THAT DURING RECONSTRUCTION OVER 2100 BLACK AMERICANS WERE ELECTED TO VARIOUS POSITIONS OF GOVERNMENT, AND REMEMBER THIS WAS THE 1800s. BY THE END OF RECONSTRUCTION THEY WERE ALL FORCED OUT AND SADLY MOSTLY FORGOTTEN.

RICHARD B. SPIKES

YOU CAN NOT RIDE IN A CAR WITHOUT THINKING ABOUT RICHARD B. SPIKES AND HIS CONTRIBUTIONS TO THE AUTO INDUSTRY. HIS CAR RELATED INVENTIONS INCLUDE: THE AUTOMATIC GEAR SHIFT, SAFETY BRAKES, AND THE DIRECTIONAL SIGNALS. HE ALSO INVENTED THE BEER KEG TAP. I REALLY DON'T KNOW WHAT THAT IS, BUT MY PARENTS OCCASIONALLY DRINK BEER, SO I'M SURE THEY WOULD BE IMPRESSED TO KNOW IT EXISTS DUE TO BLACK INGENUITY.

RAYMOND SAMUEL SCOTTRON

DID YOU KNOW THAT RAYMOND SAMUEL SCOTTRON, A BLACK INVENTOR, INVENTED THE CURTAIN ROD. EVERY TIME SOMEONE TAKES A SHOWER THEY CAN THANK MR. SCOTTRON FOR NOT ONLY PRIVACY, BUT FOR KEEPING EVERYTHING FROM GETTING WET.

ROSEWOOD

ROSEWOOD WAS A TOWN IN FLORIDA FOUNDED IN THE 1800s. IT WAS A PROUD THRIVING TOWN FILLED WITH PREDOMINANTLY BLACK AMERICANS. THEY OWNED BUSINESS, LAW FIRMS AND RAN SCHOOLS AND LIBRARIES. UNFORTUNATELY, IT WAS DESTROYED IN 1923 BY MOBS OF PEOPLE WHO SIMPLY HATED THAT THE TOWN EXISTED. I GUESS SOME PEOPLE DON'T LIKE WHEN OTHERS HAVE NICE THINGS.

RUBY BRIDGES

RUBY BRIDGES WAS THE FIRST AFRICAN AMERICAN CHILD TO DESEGREGATE THE ALL-WHITE WILLIAM FRANTZ ELEMENTARY SCHOOL IN LOUISIANA ON NOVEMBER 14, 1960. THERE WERE MANY PEOPLE THAT WERE ANGRY THAT SHE WAS THERE AND TRIED TO STOP HER. ALONG WITH THE FEDERAL MARSHALS WHO ESCORTED HER, SHE BRAVELY WALKED INTO THE SCHOOL. SHE WAS SIX YEARS OLD AT THE TIME. WHEN SHE GOT OLDER SHE BECAME A CIVIL RIGHTS ACTIVIST.

S

SARAH BOONE

SARAH BOONE GOT TIRED OF IRONING ON A BLOCK OF WOOD OR STONE, SO SHE INVENTED AND PATENTED AN IMPROVEMENT TO THE IRONING BOARD ON APRIL 26, 1892. MS. BOONE'S IRONING BOARD WAS DESIGNED TO BE EFFECTIVE IN IRONING THE SLEEVES AND BODIES OF LADIES' GARMENTS. MOST IRONING BOARDS TODAY ARE BASED ON HER CREATION.

SHIRLEY CHISHOLM

SHIRLEY CHISHOLM WAS THE FIRST BLACK WOMAN ELECTED INTO CONGRESS AND ALSO WAS THE FIRST BLACK WOMAN TO SEEK NOMINATION AND TO RUN FOR PRESIDENT.

SENECA VILLAGE

DID YOU KNOW THAT ONE OF THE FIRST SETTLEMENTS FOR BLACK AMERICANS IN NEW YORK WAS KNOWN AS SENECA VILLAGE. I'M SURE YOU ARE WONDERING WHAT HAPPENED TO IT? THOSE THAT LIVED THERE WERE FORCED OUT AND THE VILLAGE WAS REMOVED SO THAT CENTRAL PARK COULD BE BUILT. I LOVE CENTRAL PARK, BUT I'M NOT HAPPY WITH HOW THOSE PEOPLE WERE TREATED.

THOMAS L. JENNINGS
THE FIRST AFRICAN AMERICAN CREDITED TO BE GIVEN A PATENT WAS THOMAS L. JENNINGS IN 1821. AT THE TIME, PEOPLE WHO LOOKED LIKE HIM WERE NOT ALLOWED TO RECEIVE OR HOLD ONE. WHAT DID HE CREATE YOU ASK? HE CREATED DRY CLEANING. WHEN YOUR PARENTS SEND CLOTHES TO THE DRY CLEANERS, KNOW THAT IT IS POSSIBLE THANKS TO MR. JENNINGS.

TOM J. MARSHALL
TOM MARSHALL INVENTED THE FIRE EXTINGUISHER SPRINKLER SYSTEM IN 1872, WHICH IS STILL USED TO EXTINGUISH FIRES IN BUILDINGS AND LARGE FACILITIES, SUCH AS MALLS, FACTORIES, OFFICES, HOTELS AND MORE.
THOMAS ELKINS
THOMAS ELKINS IS THE INVENTOR OF ONE OF THE MOST IMPORTANT INVENTIONS OF OUR TIME. HE INVENTED THE FLUSHING TOILET. HE CALLED IT THE WATER CLOSET AT THE TIME, SINCE IT WAS WHERE ONE COULD GO AND PRIVATELY GO TO THE BATHROOM AND THEN FLUSH, ALLEVIATING THE SMELL. MY LITTLE BROTHER SOMETIMES FORGETS TO FLUSH AND I DON'T LIKE WHEN HE DOES THAT, BUT HES LEARNING. THANK YOU MR. ELKINS.

U

UNCLE TOM.

UNCLE TOM MAY SOUND LIKE SOMEONES FAMILY MEMBER, BUT IT WAS THE TITLE OF A CHARACTER IN A BOOK CALLED UNCLE TOM'S CABIN. THE CHARACTER WAS BASED ON A HEROIC MAN NAMED JOSIAH HENSON. HENSON CONTINUOUSLY RISKED HIS LIFE TO SAVE HUNDREDS OF PEOPLE BY LEADING THEM TO FREEDOM. HE LATER BUILT AND ESTABLISHED A TOWN FOR THOSE HE SAVED TO LIVE PEACEFULLY AND FREE.

I WANT TO ADD THAT...UNCLE TOM...HAS BEEN USED AS AN INSULT BY SO MANY BECAUSE THEY DON'T KNOW THE TRUE STORY. INSTEAD THEY BASE THE INSULTS ON A FEW PLAYS WRITTEN BY NOT-SO-NICE BULLIES OF HATE, WHO WANTED TO MAKE THE CHARACTER BASED ON JOSIAH HENSON LOOK BAD. THEY CREATED STORIES THAT WERE NOT TRUE , YET FOR GENERATIONS THOSE STORY DEFINED THE NAME UNCLE TOM. THE NEXT TIME YOU HEAR SOMEONE USE IT, REMIND THAT THAT ITS NOT THE INSULT THEY THINK IT IS AND THEN TELL THEM THE STORY OF JOSIAH HENSON.

V

VICTOR BLANCO
VICTOR BLANCO WAS THE BLACK AMERICAN WHO BECAME MAYOR OF SAN ANTONIO IN 1809. THIS WAS DURING A TIME THAT MOST BLACK PEOPLE WEREN'T ALLOWED TO DO ANYTHING. DURING THIS TIME TEXAS WAS STILL PART OF MEXICO AND ABOUT TO BECOME A PART OF AMERICA.
VICTOR H. GREEN
DURING A TIME OF SEGREGATION...WHEN BLACK AMERICANS DIDN'T HAVE THE FREEDOM TO GO, EAT, OR EVEN DRIVE WHERE EVER THEY WANTED TO, MR. GREENE, A POSTAL WORKER FROM HARLEM, CREATED A GUIDE BOOK KNOWN AS THE GREEN BOOK. THE GREEN IDENTIFIED AND LABELED RESTAURANTS, HOTELS, ROADS, THEATERS, AND MORE THAT WERE OPEN TO BLACK AMERICANS.

VIVIEN THEODORE THOMAS.
VIVIEN THOMAS, WITH NO FORMAL MEDICAL TRAINING, DEVELOPED TECHNIQUES AND TOOLS THAT WOULD IMPROVE BLOOD CIRCULATION IN THE HEART. HIS TECHNIQUES ARE USED IN MODERN HEART SURGERY WHICH HAS SAVED MILLIONS OF LIVES AROUND THE WORLD.
VOTING RIGHTS ACT OF 1965
THE VOTING RIGHTS ACT OF 1965 IS A LANDMARK CONSTITUTIONAL AMENDMENT WHICH PROHIBITS DISCRIMINATION IN VOTING, MAKING IT SO ALL, REGARDLESS OF RACE, CAN VOTE IN ANY AND ALL AMERICAN ELECTIONS.

W

DR. WILLIAM HINTON,

DR. WILLIAM HINTON WAS A BLACK PHYSICIAN, WHO IS CREDITED WITH CREATING A TEST TO DETECT THE SYPHILIS DISEASE.

WALTER S. MCAFEE

WALTER S. MCAFEE WAS THE AFRICAN AMERICAN MATHEMATICIAN AND PHYSICIST WHO FIRST CALCULATED THE SPEED OF THE MOON. ON JANUARY 10, 1946. HE TRANSMITTED A RADAR PULSE TOWARDS THE MOON. TWO AND A HALF SECONDS LATER, HE RECEIVED A FAINT SIGNAL, PROVING THAT TRANSMISSIONS FROM EARTH COULD CROSS THE VAST DISTANCES OF OUTER SPACE. WITH THAT KNOWLEDGE HE WAS ABLE TO CALCULATE THE SPEED OF THE MOON AND ITS ORBIT.

WILLIAM H. RICHARDSON INVENTED THE REVERSIBLE BABY CARRIAGE , WHICH WAS A HUGE IMPROVEMENTS TO THE ORIGINAL DESIGN. ALL MODERN BABY CARRIAGES ARE BASED ON RICHARDSON'S INVENTION.

WILLIAM AUGUSTIN MARTIN

HE INVENTED THE DOOR LOCK IN 1889. WHEN YOU SEE SOMEONE LOCK OR UNLOCK A DOOR,THINK ABOUT A.W MARTIN.

XAVIER UNIVERSITY

XAVIER UNIVERSITY IS A HISTORICALLY BLACK COLLEGE IN LOUISIANA FOUNDED IN 1925. DID YOU KNOW THAT XAVIER UNIVERSITY HAS ONE OF THE HIGHEST SUCCESS RATES IN THE COUNTRY FOR GETTING THEIR GRADUATES INTO MEDICAL SCHOOL. I PLAN ON GOING TO MEDICAL SCHOOL ONE DAY SO MAYBE I SHOULD ADD THAT SCHOOL TO MY LIST. ITS NEVER TO EARLY TO MAKE A LIST OR TO PLAN FOR THE FUTURE.

X, MALCOLM

WHEN I THINK OF THE LETTER "X" I CAN'T HELP BUT THINK OF MALCOLM X, EVEN THOUGH I KNOW HIS NAME STARTS WITH "M". ITS FOR THAT REASON THAT I WILL SPEAK ABOUT HIM HERE. MALCOLM X WAS A PROMINENT FIGURE DURING THE CIVIL RIGHTS MOVEMENT. REGARDLESS OF THOSE THAT TRIED TO SILENCE HIM, HE WAS ONE OF THE MOST ELOQUENT SPEAKERS AND ONE OF THE GREATEST VOCAL ADVOCATES FOR BLACK EMPOWERMENT.

YORK

YORK, WHOSE FIRST NAME IS NOT KNOWN, WAS A BLACK EXPLORER WHO JOURNEYED WITH LEWIS AND CLARK AS THEY EXPLORED THE AMERICAN WEST. YORK IS THE REASON LEWIS AND CLARK SURVIVED. HIS SKILL SET WAS VAST AND VARIED. HE HUNTED, COOKED, CREATED MEDICINE WHEN ALL FELL SICK AND WAS ABLE TO COMMUNICATE WITH INDIGENOUS NATIVES WHICH HELPED BUILD TRUST. EVEN THOUGH YORK SAVED LEWIS' AND CLARK'S LIVES MULTIPLE TIMES, THEY WEREN'T VERY APPRECIATIVE, ESPECIALLY CLARK.

Z

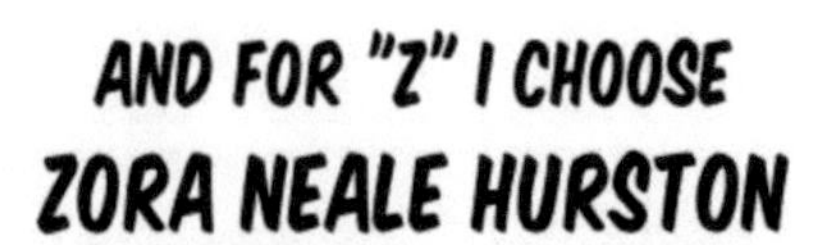

ZORA NEALE HURSTON WAS AN AFRICAN AMERICAN AUTHOR, FILMMAKER, AND ANTHROPOLOGIST. SHE IS MOST FAMOUS FOR HER BOOK "THEIR EYES WERE WATCHING GOD". HER WORK PORTRAYED THE HARDSHIPS OF AFRICAN AMERICAN LIFE IN THE EARLY 20TH CENTURY.

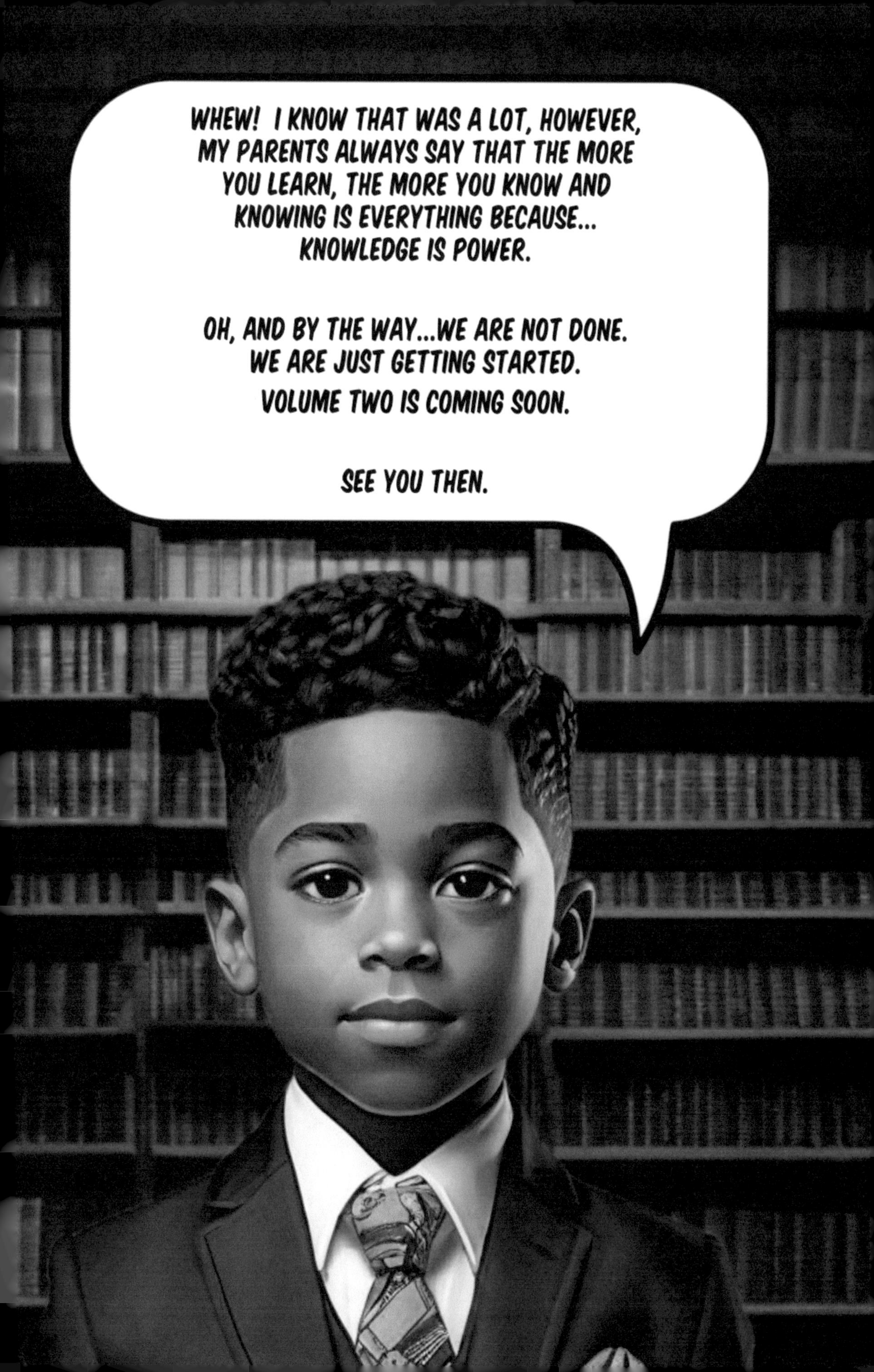
WHEW! I KNOW THAT WAS A LOT, HOWEVER, MY PARENTS ALWAYS SAY THAT THE MORE YOU LEARN, THE MORE YOU KNOW AND KNOWING IS EVERYTHING BECAUSE... KNOWLEDGE IS POWER.
OH, AND BY THE WAY...WE ARE NOT DONE. WE ARE JUST GETTING STARTED.
VOLUME TWO IS COMING SOON.
SEE YOU THEN.

Other children's books by Maurice Woodson

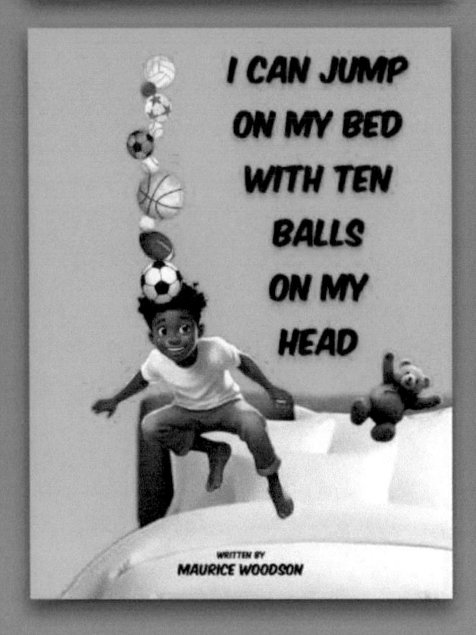

Published By MSW Books
Knowledge Is Power

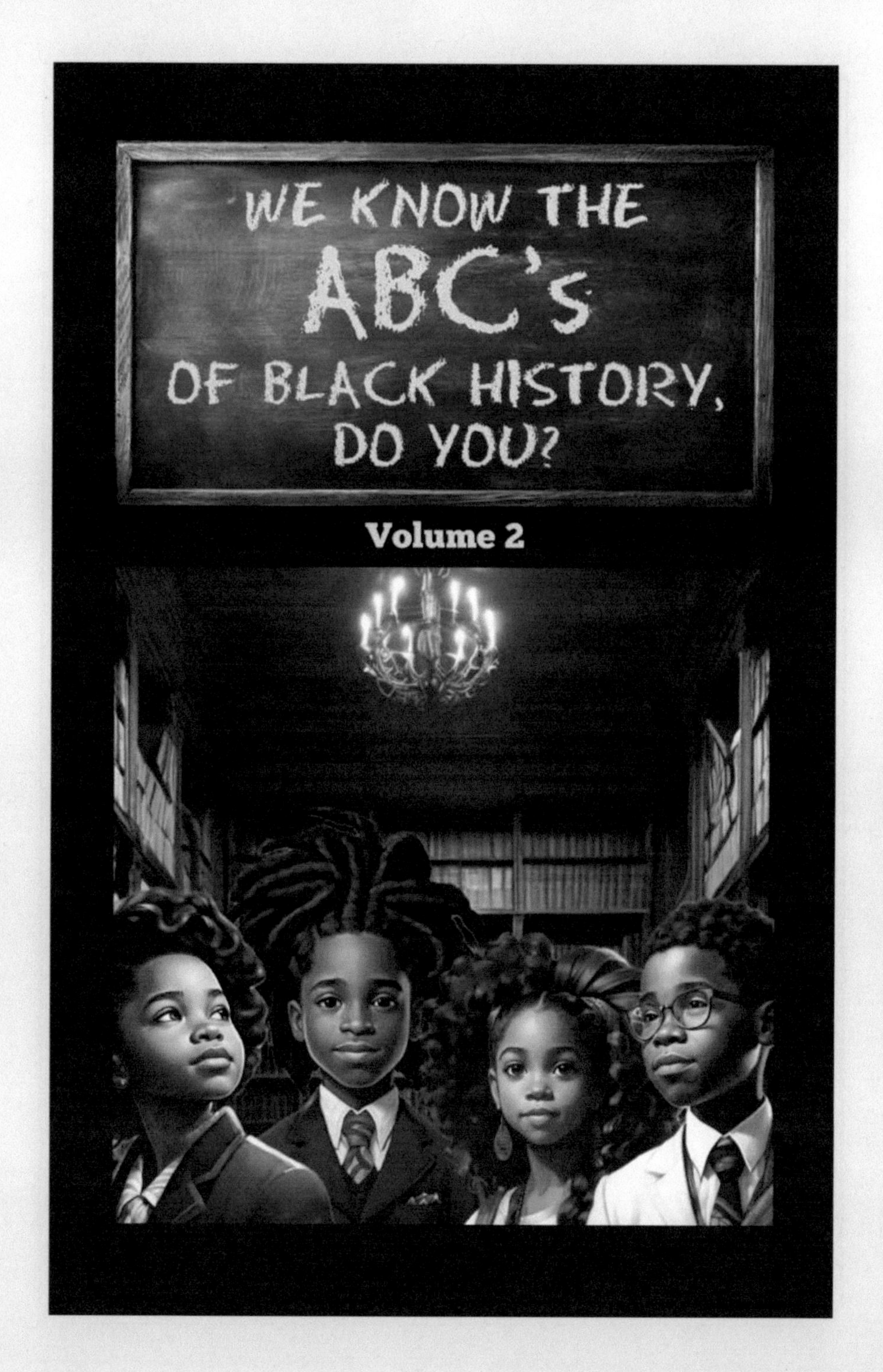
WE KNOW THE
ABC's
OF BLACK HISTORY,
DO YOU?
Volume 2

COMING SOON

Made in the USA
Columbia, SC
01 December 2024

7ae21695-6914-43b1-8bb0-c97afab6caa4R01